HER BELIEVING HEART

POEMS BY

JENNIFER POLHEMUS

Cover art by Jennifer Polhemus

ISBN: 979-8-9992568-1-2

Sligo Creek Publishing
9039 Sligo Creek Parkway
Silver Spring, Maryland
https://www.sligocreekpublishing.com/

Dedication

For Neal Michael Dwyer (1964-2025)

*We met as student and teacher, grew into friends,
and realized we were kindred spirits.*

*He opened the gates of poetry to me,
invited me into its gardens,
and then wandered away before I could whisper, thank you.*

And for James, precious James...

*who balances with me on the razor's edge
of wanting and having.
You pushed me over the cliff and I...FLEW
...and you knew I would.*

CONTENTS

Love is the only word big enough to hold everything
So that when you use it in a poem
No one hears any of the other words,
They just fill in the droning of your voice
With whatever their yearning
And all of it fits perfectly
Because all of it is true.

SECTION 1: FAMILY

A Family Narrative

Grandfather Wilfred
shot his father while hunting.
He dried up that day.

Grandfather Wilfred
loved my mother, Alice June.
Only touched her once.

Grandmother Irma
tied Mom to a kitchen chair
with a tea towel.

Grandparents carry
family sins, hand them down
like undarned wool socks.

Dad smuggled ration
coupons in dirty carpets
on his bicycle.

Nineteen thirty-six
was a hard year for little
boys looking for work.

He did not know the
tickets were there, just took his
pay and pedaled hard.

Mom would leave her four-
year-old girl with newborn twins.
Diapers are tricky.

Parents pass on sins
of families. I open
my mouth wide and bite.

Now I sell checking
accounts to people who think
they come with no fees.

Dad is so proud of
me for surviving mergers
to save customers.

He does not know that
every night I go home
and burn my left breast.

Children gobble down
family stories. Wide-eyed
we parrot them back.

A Child's Memory

Starchy and bright, the comical looking man
holds millions of bobbing balloons
green   yellow
        red
            and   blue
        He flashes a Walt Disney smile
        and August breezes blow at his hair.
        He has those marvelous puffs of helium.
She wants
        just one…one silky string
        pulled from his tangled weave lowered
        to her waiting hand much smaller than his.
She sits
        on her narrow bunk bed,
        long after the sun has set,
        with the hovering symbol of a magical day.
She pushes
        her balloon down into her lap, fiercely protecting it
        from the familiar cruelty of three older brothers.
She pretends
        she is alone, though trapped in a travel trailer
        stuffed with sweaty bodies.
She surrenders
        to their persuasion and believes their promise
        of performing a feat beyond belief
        and passes her prize to them, her innocent curiosity
        eclipsing the sick sense of danger trembling in her bones.
She watches
        them suck the life out of Mickey.
She hears
        their momentary voices squeal and laugh
        at her expense.
        They toss the shriveled Mickey by her hip
        and shuffle away as they chuckle and slap
        each other's backs.
She gathers
        up all that is left…shriveled green skin
        tied shut with thin thread falling to the floor…
        to its frayed end.

Child of Glass

Glass embedded in my 7-year-old heel and my parents yell,
Go Away! from behind the locked, dining room door
where they play cards with Carolyn and Norm
for hours and hours and endless hours.

In the bathroom, I sit, alone, alone…so silent and alone
staring at the chunky, clear shard willing myself to grab,
to pull…just pull my heart through my frightened throat,
afraid to scream or even cry. And all my unfallen tears
still try to wash away the drops of blood on the cracked, tile
floor
mixing with bits of forgotten dust and talcum powder.

So much lonely blood…running like my dreams
to hiding places where doughy arms gather me up
to bosoms of comfort, where strong hands lift me
to laps of security beyond this tiny, airless room
and me, even smaller, more breathless
then the plastic flowers in the vase of obscene white
resting, waiting, watching on top of the toilet tank.

And what do I tell my shame when it asks me
Why are you here? Why do you need? Why were you even born?
if no one was there to catch you,
to cut the cord gently and claim you,
create a new connection that glass can never sever
even when you tread clumsily on it…
scattered like diamonds across an unforgiving floor
that cries out to be cleaned to be attended to…to be loved.

House of the Ordinary Gods

Babylon is fallen, is fallen; and all the graven
images of her gods he hath broken unto the ground
~Isaiah 21:9

My mother grew up in Star Lake,
New York, fifty miles due south
of the Canadian border, where her father
hunted moose and fished for the walleyed pike.
She lived in a moody house built
from the discarded lumber of the town's
vacant hotel. The kitchen throbbed
like the heart of a shot deer and bubbled
with warmth from the wood burning stove.
On a wood floor covered with linoleum
that looked like dried pink roses, her mother,
as if she were a goddess tending frail followers,
set the round aluminum basin where the family
would bathe. She drew the curtain
between kitchen and living room
and ministered to the wide-eyed worshiper.
Her sacred right. Those rooms croaked with life
and the wood slats creaked from hushed
footsteps like crickets in June.

In town, Rubyor's was the place to go
when she was fifteen and could slip
out of a window quicker than a skink
on a sill. That particular night,
in the brooding kitchen, she fought
with her mother who chased her in
circles around the bellied stove.

No you won't go out tonight!
Yes I will!

She was in her favorite two piece
black outfit, the one with the sequins
on the blouse, and could think only
of shuffleboard and peanuts and
glances from the bar. In a frenzied
rush, her mother tore the shirt from her
body and thrust it into the smoldering stove.
Like a wiggling, crying offering to Marduk
the blouse crackled and spit on all her
hopes of escape. The kitchen grew quiet.
and my mother was forever burned
into its walls and windows and floors.

The Blackberry Serpent

Mother planted blackberries behind our house,
beyond the garage, past dad's tree nursery.
far from the shed with its rotted floor,
distant from everything I'd explored by the age of five.

When I was ten, they beckoned me,
summer globes of bloody fruit.
She said they were thornless,
but there are many kinds of thorns.
A voice came up from the dark, green tangle.
Turtle? Rabbit? Frog? No. The snake.

The whir of his words sewed up my heart with a needle.
The bleakness of bare branches
and thin clouds and my mother's crying.
We shared our family name, our eyes and quick tongues.
He coiled around my feet. wound between my legs
tasting them with his slithering licks.

Where were the blackberries of July
hot and free, dangerous and fleeting?
Their stain was almost forever, like the reputation of a bride
who gives her secret before the wedding night.

And the fruit and the leaves,
the serpent's bite, stems and thorns –
All these, abundant as banana peels,
but never enough to slip into the grave.

The Beekeeper's Daughters

Jenny? I think Dad is gone.
148 miles away and I can feel the nearness of death
dissolve in my mouth like the sandy flesh of a Christmas pear.

There will be no honey harvest late in August.
Untended hives will eventually be abandoned.
workers and drones gathering elsewhere, around a new queen.
See how busy they are dancing out locations
of other clover fields. Busy tending in the nursery.
Busy with life that always ends the same
but never quite expected.

How many times did you smoke them away
from upper frames loaded with months of sweet toil?
How many seasons saw you swaddle
their hives with tar paper and make sugar water
to sustain them through the winter?

I stay on the phone with you
until the hospice nurse arrives to pronounce him dead,
wash his body, and dress him in new, flannel pajamas.
I listen to your steady, matter-of-fact voice
describe the scene… hear the zipper's voice
trail away on the body bag.

And what is to become of us, the beekeeper's daughters
now that the caring is over and the keeper is gone?

Judah's Homeland

I.
I wonder what it's like to burn to death
in your trailer and, just for part of a second,
know that your family stands in the house
at the glass, patio doors mesmerized
by the dancing flame walls reaching up
to take oak leaves…knowing all they can do
is watch and wish and remember.
Dad rests his forehead on the cold glass.
In a voice soft and low, perhaps like King David
singing one of his love songs, his voice is clear…
>   *Where is my son?*
>   *Where is my son.*
Two daughters stand in the row.
Judah's twin watches through Down Syndrome eyes.
She is an artist, entrepreneur, self-proclaimed doctor,
Sheriff of the universe and all surrounding areas.
She sits in a dining room chair unable to watch
for reasons unspoken.
The swarm of rescue workers pours across the patio
like honeybees on a mission to find
a gathering of black locust.
One is about to open the glass door.
I pull dad back to avoid a bruising strike.
Dad's arms dangle by his sides, hands shaking.

I urge him to sit
>   *Let me get dressed.*
Mustering dignity and composure,
 he slowly walks on three legs back to his bedroom.
The female paramedic, with the perfect balance
of command and trained empathy, takes charge.
>   *Just wanted to make sure everyone is alright*
>   *or needs to go to the emergency room.*
No.

Can we just check you out?
I'm more worried about my dad, alone, in his room.
Dr. Jane, in her fascination with all things medical,
quickly raises her arm for the blood pressure cuff.
She bravely sits in silence
while they listen to her heart and lungs.
      My heart hurts.
Her wavering voice pushes out
while she rubs her upwardly stretched throat
showing her choking vulnerability.
      It's breaking.
As if I were the Ancient of Days
I reach out with my voice to embrace, reassure,
and promise what is unknown.
      Judah, my twin. He burned up.
Anger swells in my brain...pushes against my skull
like summer heat pushes away
all promise of a cool night.
Raging thoughts demand the fire fighter
to say his name... even without his dental records.
Dad dresses, lost in loss like Michelangelo
on his back, consumed by the finger of God.
I just long to float in the infinite sea
of creative, conscious energy
with my brother somewhere far off,
      But there...definitely there.

II.
Mom drifted down dementia's
silent stream. Judah waded in,
pushed against the current
desperately sure he could reach her.
He knelt to see his father's eyes
to say one more *I love you*, to beg,
Take another breath
while ribs gripped his lungs
like cage bars intent on holding
The Breath of Life, forcing it to stay
even though it's being squeezed
through unguarded spaces.

11

How many breaths does an old man have,
how far can his spine bend in on itself
when he stands before
his son's funeral pyre
separated by winter's howl
and glass doors?
I travel back exactly three months later
to see what remains of insanity's
eight-year siege against Judah.
Madness fought off by shoveling snow
falling more quickly behind Judah's forward labor
climbing into the pump house
with worn, tired tools
to catch our portion of the river beneath it,
and collecting scrap metal
for cigarettes and coffee.
I walk closely to seventeen stepping stones
curving across the lawn
like empty eyes looking for home.
I follow their searching path
to the ruins of Judah's trailer.
Torches cut the frame
into removable chunks weeks ago
leaving small, jagged pieces of insignificant
metal. Blackened earth and scattered patches
of gravel form a cruel mosaic of loss and longing.
I remember wanting to see his body;
his lipless grin,
how flames licked his flesh
the way an impatient child
consumes a lollipop
Lick...lick...CRUNCH!
Bones breaking apart at their joints.
I wanted to count his digits.
Are there still ten?
Do pinkies disappear faster than thumbs?
Judah's body vibrated back into energy.
They bagged him up and hauled him away
like passionless scientists dissecting...

disconnecting body from person.
Three cement blocks climb up to a door
no longer there.
I want to knock on that door,
go in to see his new goldfish.
Knock on that door and drag him out
of depression's cave for a cup of coffee.
Pound on that door,
scream before flames win their war.
Who will die tonight
in the wee hours of Saturday, March 5th?
Will it be as dramatic as Saturday, December 5th? Perhaps quietly
with no one knowing until sunrise.
A cloud hangs pregnant over this house, waiting to rain down death.
It's midnight. Dad labors
to capture breaths with lungs
too weak and watery to accept them.
What will the sun see tomorrow?
It will see a metal scrap
and a charred shard of sky blue ceramic
searching for the rest of itself,
sifted from the ashes,
hidden in a pocket of my jeans.

III.
Every dreaded disease
hanging from my family tree,
like early autumn apples,
has fallen into my arms.
I sit for the weight of them.
While waiting for yellow jackets, bumble bees,
and Judah's voice,
lightening bugs come with
their flashes invariably flashing.
From this tree I can see Judah's Homeland,
unwilling to receive new settlers.
Just before moon rise

I eat fruit to nothingness.
Bitter skin and sweet flesh
covered with spots and punctures,
churn and break in my belly,
gobbled up again. Too late
to leave the cut umbilical cord unclamped.
Too late to discard this body
without someone noticing,
even if only following stench
and cats crying for food by the empty bowl.
Cut it down!
It is too strong.
Rip it from the ground!
Taproot too ancient and deep.
Fruit keeps falling,
stirring in my youngest niece's womb.
Branches keep growing
up and up and out.
Every dreaded disease.
I choose not to procreate…
a gift offering to Mother Earth…
one less branch.

Soliloquy

My little sister's lungs are running out of room.
Her heart beats are lopsided.
Her compromised body
cannot withstand aggressive treatment,
and so she arrives on the doorstep
of palliative care.
not wanting to find particular phrases,
she understands in her particular way
how endings can be beautiful.

Danger and Opportunity,
the duality of crisis.
What growth is now hidden?
What healing may come?
Life is not a solitary journey.
Neither is death.

Washing Our Sister's Feet

Warm, soapy water fills the pink, plastic basin
And we search for the softest towels
In the stack brought, finally, by her tech for the night.

I have her left ankle; Ellen has her right.
Parched skin crackles against the fabric
Of her hospital socks as we gently remove them.

We each cradle a foot and her labored breathing begins to calm.
Wash away the years of dust, and toil and pain.
Dry them with the warmth of our crying smiles.

Her blue eyes cloud over and rest.
Our hands smooth lotion over her heels and soles.
Her toes remember to wiggle...like a giggle.

So weak now.
We are waiting for hospice to garner signatures,
Dot i(s), and cross t(s) so we can bring her home.
     Yes, this too is life.
     This is affirmation.
     This is her vibrant spirit.
After we slide on new, fall-risk-yellow socks,
She sinks deeper into her pillow...*Ahhh*.

Ocean City

The beach is the soul's bone
            In the winter.
            In the dark,
I listen for your breathing.
The boardwalk is more quiet
            Then you can hear.
            I listen
For your breathing in the dark.
Funnel cake tastes sweeter
            When salt is in the air.
            Your breathing
Is what I listen for in the dark.
Sandcastles stand stronger
            Mixed with ice.
            I hear
Your leaving in the dark.
I listen
To my grieving in the stark

Cold

Night.

February 16th

The wild horses of Assateague Island
Are running tonight.
Beneath a full moon,
They carry our sister home.
      We sit with her body
      Cooling now, going pale.
And the horses snort
And neigh her name.
To a mysterious and endless sea
They bring her,
Leaving the sheltered bay behind.
      Two attendants
      From Eastern Shore Cremation Services
      Cover her body
      With a green and white checkered blanket.
      We feel like a picnic on a rainy day.
And when the sun rises,
Dancing fire across the water,
We begin our grieving with patient smiles.

Making Peace

I will survive this family.
I will watch one brother in the bathtub full of bloody water.
Instead of helping him stay above the scarlet surface,
I will run into the woods and scream my joyful horror
into the first greens of spring.

I will survive this family.
I will sift through the charred remains
of the place where the youngest brother died.
Instead of weeping for the pain
of his blistering, blackened flesh and boiling blood,
I will claim a grotesquely broken chunk of pottery
as forever my own and leave him in the rubble
to search for the choices he was too terrified to make.

I will survive this family.
I will see another brother's silent body
dangling from the automatic garage door's steely machinery.
Instead of cutting him down for the sake of dignity
I will take the change from his pockets
and buy myself a treat from McDonald's dollar menu.

I will survive this family.
I will return each of their legacies, attempted, and ultimately
abandoned.
I will reclaim my body, starve and carve it into submission,
celebrate the serpent now uncoiled, and hold quiet, sacred space
for my filthiest thoughts, for my triumphant recognition.
I will lay my healing hands on my very own Divinity.

SECTION 2: WOMEN

Earth Woman

She circles in silent endurance,
a jewel at the throat of chaos.
Like a nurturing breast in midnight's nursery,
She is loved and taken for granted.

What seed waits
in her richest soil
unable to grow without her?
For she has buried it deep,
but not forgotten.

A seed which will grow
long brown hair in want of wind,
pale cotton dresses and white lace gloves
covering fingers that know secrets of herbs.

A seed which holds
promise of daughters
and miracles of sons.

A seed which remembers
how it all began –
full lipped smiles, bare feet in sandals,
and the earth, spinning free.

Prophecies

I make tea for a German woman, all the while
looking for signs. She sits on my deck,
in the clear amber air and plays her French horn.
Its metal-butter notes circle in opposition
to twinkling jumbles of my wind chimes.
Rings of the burner glow beneath my copper kettle,
water moves inside its belly. Liquid changes and rises
like an exhalation. Some of it waits for Darjeeling leaves
to flutter into boiling arms. Your music sounds like
cinnamon candy and razor blades. Its rhythms fall
into my potion and turn it a rich garnet hue, the
stone of your birth. We drink in smiling silence
as the sun gives up her fight with one final cry of color,
a long, low wail of strawberry licorice. I look
at the wet maze of leaves in my cup, a residue
foretelling me home, and close my eyes so tightly
against tears that I see veins spiral back
into my brain.

But I love you. I loved you.

Surrendering

Her hands are always last to give up the fight.
bitten fingernails, dry, painful looking splits at their tips,
like turtle bites in the flesh of a tomato that has dried in the sun,
slips of white skin peeling away from the cuticles, knuckles
swollen
from cracking, two gold rings on each finger that she uses to
explain
her contrasting dispositions. this delicate linking of bones
beneath loose skin holds a white, china bowl
filled with pecan pie and golf ball scoops of chocolate
chip ice cream. Propped up against her bed pillows
the bowl rests on her chest between the soft falling of her
breasts.
Ice cream melts – melts – melts. Her eyelids flutter – flutter –
close.
The bowl tips and threatens to spill, but her left index finger
is bent over the edge like a steadfast hook in a fish's mouth.
Right hand forgets to hold the spoon and her pinkie
slides into the chilly puddle of sweetness.

She is dreaming.
She is the rising swell
of a ski slope in Austria.

My love, why don't you let yourself sleep?
I lift her right hand and lick warm milk from her fingers.
She turns her head and gives up the bowl whispering,
I don't want you to leave me.

Cat Puzzle

Fran fans her hand through puzzle pieces
in a box on a table in the community dining room.
She is so small compared to the other patients
who stop by to place a piece or two.
The table is too damn small, she says in group therapy,
like my window ledge above the kitchen sink.
This is where her cat, Reader, folded his black body
and tucked white paws on sunny days.
The edges are almost done, and she sips tepid water
from a clear plastic bottle, trying to cool down
from her walk after lunch. Sweat dampens
the short, silver hair at her temple and nape,
turning it a gleaming gray like polished granite.
Her legs echo the shape of a dancer's.
Sometimes Michael sits with her and sorts pieces by color.
He is from Italy. She likes that. Her eyes glide back and forth
over the emerging picture of cats, the same way she used to look
for Reader's tail as he hid under the bed in the front room.
This one looks just like his eye, she whispers to herself.
She holds it tightly for many minutes.

A Gentle Undoing

We met when honeysuckle bled from its vine
in the sweaty air of a June night.
When apple walnut muffins waited in a vine and reed basket
I wove between the tears,
before our voices spilled over into memories.

I found you as an open hand hell bent on caressing my face
and back handing my heart until I fell back, weightless,
voluntarily consumed into the knowing of you.

You waited for me at an Exxon station
sitting on a curb in the parking lot,
chain smoking, contemplating the moral differences
between spontaneity and impulsiveness.

Which of us knew that rising each morning
would be our greatest challenge
or sleeping together beneath the night
with only the residue of dreams, a triumph?

Dreams that haunt us, compel us, save as they destroy us,
birth us into oblivion, pull us back, and throw us in
fill our heads with pictures unfit to keep for their sake
and wash our hearts with blood and fire and moonlight.

This is how we met and this is how we live,
in a desperate dream, a gentle undoing of our senses.

I Have Told You Everything

Can I be honest with you, Carol, and all the lesbians between
us?
Although some of them were bi or straight
like Kate, with her obsidian thigh that broke in two.
We'd laugh as she dressed in a bedroom
on the second floor of my parent's house,
neither of us realizing that I was watching
how her breasts hung in emerald satin cups.

Or Marcia, who let me drink beer off her nipples
while Patrick fucked her, but never came,
in fear of fathering a retarded child.

Or the first Carol who should have known, but I didn't.
Pieces of her still wait like frightened animals
in a box at Iron Forge Storage
next to our Christmas decorations and camping equipment.

You know their names
                faces
          dates
places.
The particular twist of their knives,
promises that lie in their eyes
and the way I crept like English ivy up their red brick walls
when their mouths where full with my name.
I have told you everything except the truth.

Not a Big Loss

Fifteen years later
I dropped my wedding band
down the heat vent in the
bathroom floor. It slipped
like a coiled snake
from my still shrinking finger.
I was not sad or desperate,
only afraid of your screams
and fists, the sparse blades
of my hair tugging back
against the cage of your fingers.
You said you could retrieve it.
You have said many things
succulent and sharp.
Brought many gifts,
a bouquet of terror
and the razor's edge of roses.
The promise of a super nova
reined in by a circle of metal.
Not a big loss, just brass
blessed in holy rosemary water
ten days after they were shipped
from Fingerhut to our apartment
before our house in the 'Hood.

Sweet Basil and Marmalade

Rebecca sits in her wheelchair at the kitchen counter.
She still has strength to chop oranges and lemons.

Sugar boils around the acid jewels
and yields three pints of Rebecca's last days.

Lacey harvested herbs from the garden last week.
Another season over as frost creeps along the valley.

Tonight, she lifts sweet basil from a hook on their kitchen wall
and pulls each curled, brittle leaf from its woody stem.

Their bed is in the dining room now.
Rebecca cannot make it up the stairs anymore.

Lacey's potions of olive oil, flax seed and rosemary
smell of life, but they cannot break life's promise of death.

Lacey saves the stems. They'll make good weavers
and ribs for spring's empty willow baskets.

Sluice

I want to plant an herb garden of my own,
behind our house, where you dug soil
for your potted tomato plants
that yielded three diminutive pink rocks.

I want to rip into the earth
with a heavy, metal hoe
plunge the tines of a forked spade
deep, to release the soil
from its clods, throw aside
the stones and rocks,
the unforgiving hardness
of undeveloped dirt.

I want to nurture rosemary,
mint, and cilantro. Perhaps
some lemon basil or garlic.
Where the rain drops into gutters,
drips down a chalk-white
aluminum downspout, splashes
and splatters against a
floating, plastic cradle,
Diverted and seeping into my shaded garden.

Gift

All I have left, physically, of Grace Wells
is a sparse collection of tattered, Little Golden Books
carried with me lovingly, even fiercely, to rented basements,
back home again and again. To lovers' houses in a state almost
as green
as I imagine Ireland to be – less the faeries, of course.
To new places, after the violence, of self-hewn solitude and
safety.

Grace lived in a house in the woods, with a grand porch.
As I remember, not a far drive from my parents' home.
She brought a Little Golden Book to church for me
on scattered Sundays full of anticipation.
Developers cut down many of her precious trees
one autumn – and built a McDonald's.
Still, she gifted – or entrusted? into my eager hands – or mind?
one Little Golden Book at a time.

We went to her home once – or many times?
with lace-edged linens in paper-lined drawers,
each with a pine-scented sachet, and years that poured over her
like bobby pins and clothes lines. Like gingerbread trim
on peaks above windows that chipped and grayed and cracked.
And still, Little Golden Books found their way to me,
delivered, as a deer bears a fawn in the spring.

One time, as I recall – long ago now –
the county tore down Grace's house and replaced it
with a parking lot where commuters waited for buses.
And the Little Golden Books never came again,

For Marietta

Marietta begins to speak.
Her voice is like the whispering of angels
and her hands eternally seek something to hold.
Her eyes gaze back across decades,
over a valley filled with pain only God can understand.

She speaks to me of community, insanity,
fathers, Canada, 1967, double pneumonia,
and mothers rocking empty blankets.

She speaks to me of her daughter, Ellie,
and Ellie hangs there in a tear
on Marietta's cheek, not ready to leave.

I kiss her forehead.
Cool perspiration clings to my lips
in a thin covering sheet,
like Ellie's mood on a sunny day.
God is good. And He answers prayers
in a way only Marietta can know.

Marietta has come to me with the measured step of seasons,
like maple blossoms burning red
and half-moon pushing its belly against a purpling sky.
She comes to me and I hold her face in my hands,
touching a place only my spirit can remember.

The Comma,

I am not here to annoy you,
Or to destroy you,
I am here only asking you,
To pause,
To take one small breath,
And remember,
What has gone before,
And anticipate,
With curious celebration,
What lies ahead,
The possibility of perfection,
When everything withers,
Around you,
And refuses,
To fall away,
Only clings and clings,
And desperately clings,

Remember,
That I started as a period,
An exhausted ending,
That was not ready to go,
And when the world refused to end,
A casual,
Yet conscious stroke was added,
The universe rested,
For an unmeasured moment,
And then continued,
The sacred dance,
Continue,
Continue,
Begin again,

Almost Spring

Winter still strokes the ground with her frigid fingers.

In an arrogant, artsy, and small college town sits a park
where she hid Kelly, her bike.
Farther away, in abrasive bushes, low to the ground,
she hid her body and waited.

While her body was dying, she came to me
in my ordinary bedroom wearing nothing particularly
memorable.
Standing two feet above my floor, she quickly paced
from corner to corner, landing each hurried footstep on air
while she frantically wrung her dirty, scratched hands.
She asked, maybe herself, maybe not,
What do I do? ...turn...pace...wring...*What do I do?*

When her body was almost dead, she came to me
at work and stood two feet above and just behind
my office chair while I sat at my desk and listened
to my coworker recount all those we had lost to suicide.
She stood there, wearing panels of black crepe, satin, velvet, and
silk
stitched together crudely. Long tatters moved almost
imperceptibly
at the sleeves and hem. Her long, dark brown hair hung
from her slightly bowed head, covering her face,
in thin, strangling tangles. It was so full with grease and filth
that it shined in the florescent light, almost black.
I don't want to hear about any more dead people, Richard.
He stopped and casually leaned back in his chair
crossing one leg over the other.

When her body was finally dead, she came to me
at the meeting my boss held in her cramped office
where she announced to five employees squished into a circle of
chairs,
She is dead.
While they cried or squirmed in their seats

or looked ahead with open-mouthed stares,
She stood beside and two feet above my boss' chair
wearing a simple, white, cotton-knit dress
bursting with tiny flowers in yellows, reds and blues –
the smaller leaves not forgetting to be green.
Her hair was bobbed short against her jaw.
It almost bounced against her motionlessness,
full and thick and warm. The workers talked
about much and said even less. She and I
breathed a satisfied sigh and smiled fondly at them all.

When her body burned into ashes, she came to me
in my truck on my way home from work.
Sat right in the front seat. Sat exactly next to me.
Even remembered to wear her seatbelt.
This time, I could just barely catch the scent
of her white, cotton-knit dress with flowers.
It smelled like a piece of spring. I could see
the corner of her smile and her eyes looking forward
and the drape of her almost plump, freckled arms falling
to the hands resting in her lap. I could perceive her entire
silhouette
without even turning my head. I said to her,
out loud to make sure we both heard,
You need to go now.

She hasn't come since, but then again, I haven't let her.

Called Home

I sit on a toilet in a stall
exactly the same as the nine others in this women's restroom
exactly the same as the three women's restrooms on this hospital
floor
exactly the same as the forty other women's restrooms in this
hospital building
exactly the same as the hundreds of women's restrooms on this
hospital campus
this Mecca of health and death
for thousands of American Veterans.
On the back of this stall door is a blood-red flyer
trying to convince women they deserve a healthy relationship.
There are ten tear-off tabs on the bottom of the flyer
with the number for the National Domestic Violence Hotline.
                    And they all were called home.
June ripped the first one from its place that seemed forever far
away.
She snatched it like a frightened mouse
taking with it a long tear up the side of the flyer
and stuffed it into the left hip pocket of her purple scrubs
on her way back to the Radiology Department where she
registers
another quivering old man who struggles to hold still for his
MRI.
                    And they all were called home.
Tamika carefully removed the second tab for her mother
and the third, a bit more roughly, for herself
and for her daughter and for generations to come
for the splendid, empty-eyed women marching in the past
forever marching
until the beat of their feet drove Tamika sane.
                    And they all were called home.
And the fourth one, that one was removed from the far side
with determination, even reverence.
She is an artist. Her father rescued an orphan in Saigon
and felt his wife's last breath in his face
with his hands crushing her bursting, silent throat.

This artist, this goddess, this witch, this queen took the far right
tab from every stall
in every women's restroom
on every floor
in every building
on that hospital campus.
She worked with paint and metal and stone
She worked with feverish, orgasmic energy...the most powerful
energy of all
the energy of Creation.
She laid and pressed and folded and scrunched and pushed and
choked and cut and slapped
every tear-off tab into
her art
her idol
her statement
her scream
And she worshiped it with her sacred circle of women
naked...in the forest...in the darkness blessed by fire
                              And they all were called home.

Sisterhood of the Traveling Tissues

I have no words to soothe you, sister golden hair.
Only this small packet of tissues
given to me earlier today, when it was new,
by a goddess of guns, slid across yet another table tonight.
Two are gone now, full of my tears fallen from eyes
that watched a brother burn, a heart longing to die,
and finger's bones worked breathless for a dream.
Take them, since I am still here,
let them catch your sobbing questions
that Ryan will never hear because he died too soon to answer
them
too late to say you were his friend. Do not give them back to me
until the packet is empty. As empty as your heart
that tries to believe he is gone.
Gone, like I will be on my birthday, eased into endless sleep.
Giving up whispers and flesh and promises.
Finally feeling magnificent enough
to recover what should have been mine to begin with.
I give it all to you sweet, innocent Ella,
with your shorn hair laying in heaving chunks around your feet.
Would you have still cut it if you knew "goodbye"
would be as difficult to say as "I am sorry"?
And in your aching travels you will meet another wandering
heart,
chest laid open, revealing her beating, bloody pain.
There will be just enough tissues left to soak up all her heavy
life.
It is a bitter miracle then, what one packet of tissues can hold,
passed among sisters and thrown into urgent baskets of waste.

Margaret's Spider

I watched a spider outside my window
                Refused to go down to the dining room
She weaved a web…it took days
                A man came to visit…I didn't know his
name…he kept calling me Mom
Then she spun a cocoon around herself
                The man brought a floral quilt…he said I made it
After a long while…hundreds of tiny spiders emerged
                They put a tube down my nose
They each floated…drifted away
                I fell out of my bed yesterday
On a single, silky filament
                And crawled back in before they noticed
The Mistress Spider never reappeared
                Tiny fractures mosaiced across my hips
And I watched for her
                As the pain drowned out my dreams
I watched…until I died

Sitting in the Mystery

As she tells me her story of brokenness
I realize I am hovering in the aboves and belows of
consciousness
where my own heart releases me from blindness,
from bondage in Past and Future and casts my truth onto the
shores of Now,
This Sacred Moment.

Shadow and light share their quantum dance
in an autumn meadow, naked, under a waxing gibbous moon.
I can feel my life mysteriously calling
as I watch my dreams and who I thought I would be
turn to dust.

I look into her eyes then, so full of emptiness,
swallowed by an anger that devours all other emotions
and know that my magic-making
my devotions and potions, words in whispers,
strings of energy looping us together
as the Serpent Goddess coils up my spine,
crosses over yours where the third eye looks upon our
genderlessness,
and our venom alchemizes into an elixir
offering the fearful comfort of Nothingness.
There is a queer beauty in silence that floats like diadems
around my crown and down my arms,
drips from my fingers
into the endless pool of another day.

A Love Note to Knikki

Like a riverbed on the moon
feeding the Sea of Tranquility,
you have not forgotten ancient waters
flowing with a thousand reflections
running deep with myriad souls.
One of them was mine.
You chose not to hold me captive
and allowed me to evaporate
into air
       and clouds
              and become down pours
forming puddles and pools,
lakes and oceans of my own
all bearing your infinite, invisible mark,
the essence of your sacred signature.

I am pulled back to your banks
to stand in witness of you again.
To celebrate your beauty, wisdom, and power
etched on your stones
abundant on your lunar landscape
still lush and juicy
like a Royal Womb ready to create,
We are Feminine Divine.

SECTION 3: MEN

This Passion

Eight gossamer wings beat out a tale of
one illicit passion. Bound in soil-scented air, both
ate from vines in a rock-walled garden.
For release, they sought an oracle's word, and in
six quarter moons they became gods. Now, along stone
eight feet high, rough and cold, they struggle
to feel their souls through the braille on walls they have built.

Phases

You are like the moon,
pulling my watery thoughts
to a distant place
then pushing them back
before they are completely free.
But I am deeper
than your glassy face
will ever see.

Before You, There Was Mr. Rogers

Three years old and toddling at my mother's hem,
Her swollen belly grants me shade from a blistering,
metropolitan sun.
We walk streets that are strange to me, climb stairs I never
dreamed existed,
and enter a fearsome door that creaks with promises of
abandonment.

She plopped me down with other diminutive creatures.
After not too many minutes I stopped looking over my left
shoulder
to comfort myself with her ponderous presence.
Too much time…too much…too much
Passes between alphabet blocks and her…and me.
She was gone…no surprise to me.
Wicked children never get to keep their mommies.

Before you came with your growl and itchy hide,
Mr. Rogers told me, with an even-toned smile,
that he liked me and I was his friend.
It was enough…
enough to believe my way to your doorstep.
enough to keep my innocent secret safe.
Enough…enough…and breathlessly…enough.

When I met you I came to understand
Neighbor and the puppeteer's magic
in the Land of Make Believe.
Everything was make believe
until you.

Hierophant

My dreams are fitful and full of you.
With costume parties and roaming down streets
in clumps of threes hurrying home to you
before you even arrive. I am fifteen again,
sitting in the back of the classroom
writing poems with you, line by torturous magnificent line.
And suddenly politics are urgent
as if the New British were coming
as if AI were a chip in our brains,
much more than tertiary cognition we hold in our hands.
And art is the flavor of honey and quinine,
forcing us to suck our thumbs
and recoil…disgusted.
And intellectuals retreat to the dark web
where there is voice and reason spun with tears.
And in every birthday wish there are numbers,
bell curves, and sacred geometric objects
spinning free on X, Y, and Z.
And it is all so good!
The radiant, voracious smorgasbord
of you
and me
and we.

Two Bottles of Cheap Sangria Later…

No, I don't know what forever means
and my definition of an open relationship
changes at least twice a day.
Yes, we can fit all our things
in a one bedroom apartment
and yes, it will look like you live there too.
I won't give up my books
or my cassette tapes.
What do you mean by asking me that?!
I still have a cassette recorder.
Yes, it works!
I don't know why I cry sometimes
after we make love. And what
kind of question is that to ask a Queen?!
I do know one thing;
I'm drunk. Let me sleep.

Oh, one more thing,
I love you more than sleep,
and definitely more than cheap sangria.

For Boompa

Forty years ago, you gave me a paper bag
full of all that life can offer. I squandered it
not knowing a thin sack of dried wood pulp
could hold such wonder, such despair
such promise of something more
something wholly other, something quietly sacred
shared between us on this humid Monday
over an invisible wave bounced between steel towers.

You do not like that you are dying, and I hate it.
And I promise you this day to meet hatred with compassion
greed with generosity and ignorance with wisdom.

I thought to bury the bag with you.
I have decided to keep it, to fill it up again with your spirit,
the sound of tinkling bells from the caravan
that passes below your window one final time.

You leave me with stardust in my eyes
and a garden ripe for harvest.
I will eat fruit straight from the vine,
warmed by the sun and washed with my tears.
Yes, I will bite the flesh deeply, let juices drip from my chin,
fatten me for the winter to come, howling and dark and long.
And spring will come again. It always does.
For this, for all of this, I lift my face in gratitude.

There is Such a Thing

There is such a thing as the sunrise in your eyes
on the winter solstice
in a cave that did not fill with light
because clouds hung thick and threatening.
I turned to you and talked about hockey
and what made it different than soccer.

There is such a thing as a line of poetry
that evokes the scent of a garland in your hair
and the sound of a supernova in the sway of your hips.
I sit too far away from you
to see the hole in the seam of your dress
and the skin not so far beneath,
yet within my brain the image is conjured
and trickles down my throat
into my chest that twitches.
I speak to you of classrooms full of blank faces,
ears that hear but do not listen,
and hearts that have forgotten what compels them to beat.

I do not intend to be a voice of wisdom. I just tell stories.

Trauma Twin

I touch the hot coal
you harbor in your belly.
I know it intimately.
It is the mirror image of mine.
I know its heat,
the way it burns
through the flesh of every lover
and even worse,
every friend
who could have been more.

I gaze into the shimmering root
of that dancing flame
and whisper the secret
to extinguish it
just loud enough
so that neither one of us can hear.

The Picture

I don't like opening a book
and finding a memory
of the first woman I ever loved with all my heart.
A collection of Ginsberg sat on my shelf
for twenty years.
One forgotten night, I pried open its yellowing pages
and you came tumbling out.
And my tears came tumbling down.
I remember you, grandma.
I was twelve
and you were the most beautiful creature I'd ever seen
at midnight
in my suffocating room
and you held me more than tight
less than tired
until my fever broke
into pieces of life that fell all around you,
below your disheveled hair and searching eyes,
the softness of your arms and the hem of your nightgown.
Spilled over the callouses on your lovely feet
and rested on the eternal ground
that cracked and begged for water
For a moment I'd forgotten just how much I miss you.

Wearing the Light

When shadows threaten to choke me, you offer,
Light comes in direct proportion
to how much you allow darkness
to flow through
We speak of sacred embracing and being a living love story.
And amidst the swirl of shadows, sunbeams come through the window
behind your right shoulder. The rays approach you silently,
yellow and white and bright…almost deafening,
creep over your back and cradle you.
And you do not realize they are holding you,
defining your questioning edges,
anointing you into your magnificence.
I am the only one who sees it,
drinks in its deliciousness and calls it my own.
And in my mind I float around you
within the beams, like dust
dull and sparkling all at once.
I decide to reveal to you what I see
and you shrink away from the light.
Why, Osho? Why?
Why do you pull away from your divinity
when I am the one witnessing it,
taking refuge in my own perception of you?
It is not you I am perceiving. It is me. It is us. It is all of us. It is Oneness.
Please let me have this. Give me the gift of validating my own reality
so that I can offer it up to Emptiness
and find comfort, find peace.

I Who Am, Who Am I?

I.
I am the spaces in between,
the breath exhaling,
and the earth coming up to meet it.
The heart seeking sanctuary
and the stars smiling down to embrace it.
The mind trembling in the dark
and the fear awakening to its own delusion.

I am YOU sitting here next to ME
not knowing what to say or do,
bearing witness to suffering,
and allowing wisdom to emerge
from the chrysalis of compassion.

II.
What do I say when your eyes search my face
for a sign of understanding?
When you look into me, beyond my mind,
and pose your question
to the emptiness filled with love.
When your howling *Why?*
echoes through the canyon of my soul
and returns as a whisper
that falls like a feather at your feet,
or a fading sonata
that vibrates from a wounded cello.

I say
Tell me more.
Show me the hurt
that wilts the flowers you lay on the grave.
Sing me the song that began as a lullaby,
ended in a wall of noise that crumbled into laughter,
and was hauled away in a hearse.
Remember me the memory of Sunday brunch
and fevered nights that break into mornings
where doves scour the rubble for survivors,
and find only worms…and words.

III.
Yes,
I am the moment just before grief
and the eternity after it.
I am the truth all the stories tell
and the moon to which the finger points.

SECTION 4: ONE MAN IN PARTICULAR

Key to the Realm

Long before I met you,
when you were hidden away in your castle
of stone and flame and tapestries,
I strung a strand of prayer beads…
Tibetan, wood beads…painted red and gold.
For the guru bead, to join the ends
to create the circle
that holds The Power
Yes.
For that final bead,
instead of a cross nailed to my heart with silence,
I chose a heavy, brass skeleton key
refusing to be polished,
scarred with tiny gouges that are there, yet barely noticed.
Yes.
They are forever there.
Yes.
Instead of a cross, I tied the key
and cut the frayed, loose ends.
It was done,
and I did not understand why I made it.
It remains done and it remains incomplete.
Heaving an unsettled and accepting sigh,
I laid it on my altar…where it collected dust for years,
Yes.
For years it rested beneath a shroud of dust
waiting patiently…gently…whispering.
Murmuring…until I could hear.
Yes.
Waiting…for me to remember.
When I finally met you,
when I came seeking sanctuary from the storm,
you pierced my armor through and through
with your azure blue eyes…Then you smiled.
You lead me to your throne room
with its consuming, life-sustaining central fire.
Yes.

You lead me to your throne room.
I listened to the softness of your robe trailing long behind.
You offered me a chair at your Great Table.
Everyone is there.
Yes.
All of us are here.
When I lifted my weary eyes to meet yours
I stumbled, almost falling, into Peace.
It was then that I heard the quiet calling of the key.
I lifted it from my altar.
Yes.
I brought it to my bosom and filled it with holy intention.
Yes.
I consecrated it for The Journey.
I cradled the key in my cupped hands
and extended it towards you.
Yes.
Reached across the Void to give it to you
knowing I was home.
Yes.
Home.

The Hunt

I catch the scent of you
drifting over the African veldt.
I have come for water.
This lioness is thirsty, so thirsty
and desperately aware
that you are near, that the hunt has begun.
Restless and wanting, weaving between bushes
waiting to catch a glimpse of you
I pant out my desire
claw the ground, prepare for the chase.
My paws pound the Earth in rhythm with my beating heart.
This is hungry work and I want to be caught
to hear the clicking cock of your mighty gun
feel the wildness of your controlled shot
explode into my flesh, unyielding and taking
falling beneath you, surrendering to your conquest.
My pleasure bleeds out around you.
Keep my pelt for the warmth of memories
and mount me on the wall of your heart
to forever watch over you.

Captured

I tilt my head to lay a kiss on your neck.
I can feel the pulse of your blood
rushing beneath my lips,
hurrying back to your heart.

My lips lace their way to catch your earlobe.
I can hear the jostling tinkle of my earrings.
The delicate motion of a chorus of tiny metal leaves
cascading
impatiently caressing your shoulder
that lifts your arm
that guides your hand
that pushes your fingers
into my hair
and clenches.

I whisper.
My mouth is a breath away from your ear
and my cheek presses against yours.
I whisper
     You have me
breath
     Now
breath
     Do what you will

Sensing

Do you know what it is like to be found…
by someone who listens with their soul
and not just their ears?

Do you know how it feels to find…
a piece of writing that moves your belly
and not just your eyes?

It is like hearing the day breaking
out of the cold shell of night.

It is like watching the moon rising,
pushing the searing sun away.

It is like smelling salt and sand
at the end of the Oregon Trail.

It is like touching the birth-wet skin
of your first child.

It is like tasting the wanting kiss
of the lover you meet, at last,
after an endless exchange of impassioned letters,
communicating with lips and tongues
in the secret, sacred language of longing
and promise of redemption.

It is like my hand finally finding its way
to rest on your chest, feeling your heartbeat
as I whisper, almost plead,
Make me believe again.

It is like you there, and me here
connected by the web of energy
in which we are caught,
suspended in gossamer filaments
of yearning and desire, hopes and dreams,
prayers and spells, while the spider of synchronicity
creeps along the weave creating delicate vibrations
that we both sense, that murmur of impending transformation.
It will be consumption, transubstantiation, then transcendence…
a theoeroticism where flesh and blood become ambrosia and
nectar,
feeding the hunger that brought us to this place,
from believing to knowing.

These Things...

These things are dreams...
a college campus
a quantum entanglement of hearts
a mindset of abundance in a sea of lack
fudgesicles
and cherry cobbler with no pits.

These things are memories...
a red bean bag chair
a muscular thigh with dark hair
a garage loft covered in dirty chunks of green carpet
pig tails
and a window with no panes.

These things are real...
a Jedi creature kept close
the taste of you before dinner
spending the weekend for no other reason than me
promises
and sent emails with no answers.

These things are now...
the moment that finally comes
the way I look at you and you look back
showers together when there is nothing left to be dirty
heartbeats
and windows left open, on purpose.

Sacred Union

The weaving of the dharma of our souls
began beneath the cover of October skies,
when I needed nothing from you
and you needed nothing from me.
Yet we gave everything completely.
We embarked on an uncertain journey
to a certain destination on a shared horizon.
An ultimate sensuality…a mutual embodiment
fueled by a full *Fuck Yes!* embracing ecstasy,
liberating the sparks from broken vessels
laying in shards at our feet,
watching them rise like fireflies above a field
at dusk…in summer…hanging in the scent of jasmine.
And when our flesh joins in sacred union,
we will never return to seeing anything as ordinary.
The clarity will sear our hearts together.
We implode into each other…breathless.
And when I am standing at the sink washing dishes
you cannot help yourself…you must press your pelvis against
me,
wrap your arms around my waist,
take in the scent of my hair,
and light a kiss on the back of my neck
hoping it will send shivers down my spine
that end in a trickle between my legs
keeping me in a constant state of desire.

Lover

Be my moon.
Light the darkness of the forest in which I wander.
Lead me to the day where white blossoms fill apple trees
with their pink-throated centers.
Promise me that the sun is what your frigid face reflects
and do not forget to drag the stars with you,
like fire beacons, when you spin…when you fall
away from my comfort and your protection no longer affords…
And for now, for this moment
frozen in the impenetrable glacier of my life
let me find you there, at the crest of my secret hill,
hanging swollen on your ginger rising,
an illusion of stillness.
Sing a song for me or dance with new steps around the
exhausted earth.
Whatever you do, do it now…I beg you…before I forget you.

My Offer

Broken things love beauty.
The way a deer dies on the road
and a sunset explodes red across the sky.
The way I smile at you when you are not there,
believing you can see me through the darkness
that weighs down on my frightened chest
expecting miracles from shards of glass
and three smooth stones gathered silently from a stream bed.

Broken things remember that the right questions
are far more important than the wrong answers.
That *Do you love me?* holds more promise
than the answer *No.* or, worse yet, *Only if....*
That negative energy is the easiest to detect
and high vibrations are elusive in their vitality.

Broken things never miss the innuendo.
The way a poem leaves you wanting.
Like this one.

Like the Juice of Summer Melons

When the feeling of a hand caressing your cheek distracts you
from your work,
it is me.

When the longing ache to return home grips your belly,
it is me.

When the sound of geese flying southward circles your heart,
it is me.

When the thought of warm, buttered syrup drizzles over the
layers of your mind,
it is me.

When your breath catches in your throat as the image of red lips
flashes before your eyes,
it is me.

When the juices of summer melons drip down your chin sticky
and sweet,
it is me.

Yes.

I am the dream that wakes you
the thought that shakes you
the lust that overtakes you
the absence that makes you
want me.

Yes.
It is me.

I Feel You

This day closes in on me
and I can hardly move.
The mighty sun sets
its fiery foot on my neck
and I can barely breathe.
The night falls
in a thousand broken promises
that settle like stars
gasping their last
around my lost steps.
All there is left to say
swims behind our eyes
searching…searching…searching
for a way back to the sea
to primordial waters
that birthed us in one, great orgasmic thrust
onto this ancient shore…together
with no other way to find each other
than our own groping, primal scent.
So good night, my love
in your faraway place.
Never doubt for one moment
that I am coming
like a wave of eternal energy
settling in beside you again.

Did You See It?

The moon... hanging in the night sky
like a lidless eye
white and watching.....witnessing
our discrete licentiousness
our secret, sacred mind fucking.
We lay bare our brains
ooze energies
in hidden rooms of insatiable intimacy.
We collide and elide
and inhale the madness the mayhem the mystery.
I trace the curl of your lip
you, the curve of my hip
with searching, famished fingers
hungry for flesh and bone and blood
that rips and breaks and bleeds,
that breathes into bellies full of seed,
that bathes in fluids forbidden, then forgotten
only to wake, as we writhe in our lust
like salmon swimming, leaping towards home
born of a thought that flowed into a feeling
becoming a whispered prayer to gods laid in ruins
beneath the moon
the moon
the moon
white and watching

Reflections

This year found me feeling the crystalline energy
of our unique, alchemical magic.
At times, my whole third eye opened
as a rainbow diamond of infinite cravings
and possibilities
and the joy of expanded horizons.
When you were lost in the storm
from summer to fall,
I let myself shatter on the sharp mystery of life.
I allowed my heart to break
because most things
need to break before they can grow.

Heartbreak is the poetry of life,
and through its lines,
my hopes and dreams and desires are healed
and made more than the whole they were
before the fragmentation.
Yes, sometimes I feel more cracked than mosaic
and only recognize my beauty
when I hover high above it.

And if we are not heartbroken,
then we are not paying attention
because the brokenness is the guarantee
that we live in a universe that wants
so much more for us than normality.
It wants us to see beauty everywhere,
and that we are here to make our way
to enlightenment.
Heartbreak is the signature of a universe
that wants our wisdom
more than it wants our happiness.

This year,
I showed up for the celebration
and the tears,
allowed life to make and remake me
into the shape of wisdom.
I found that sometimes
the universe makes all my dreams come true,
and sometimes it crushes them
so I can find truth
in the reflection of my own puddles of tears.

Joy and heartbreak are lovers
that dance together in my soul,
moving in synchronous rhythm
creating the embodiment of courage.
They dance, like we do,
embrace moments that erupt out of ordinary days
become burning engagements
that spill over into memories that flow
like lava down the sides of our mountain
of special needs and hidden wants.

Hugs and magic and mischief to you
through space and time

Hungry Ghosts

I am now aware that I am greedy for you
like clinging to a gigantic rock hurtling through space
around a tremendous fireball, and not knowing why.
This greed has spilled over into hatred
like plucking a pristine lily from our nurturing pond
only to let it rot in a vase on my bedside table.
And this hatred, this greed, is fueled by the delusion
that I actually understand questions for which there are no
answers.
I allowed myself to crave you like an animal in heat.
To devour you like a starving tigress on the hunt
for flesh and bone and blood.
All of this brought suffering as my heart closed in on itself
and my eyes saw something I thought I recognized,
a heart that was never there.
I thought I heard it pounding…almost reached out and touched
it…
dared to hold it as my own…but you had not offered it.
All I found there were days full of emptiness,
nights glutted with dreams that melted from memory
long before I could interpret them, unravel their symbols,
and search for prophetic patterns.
The only way to feed these hungry ghosts,
greed, hatred, and delusions, is to swallow them whole
with generosity, compassion, and wisdom.
Let them churn in my belly and sustain me,
give me strength to embark on an uncertain journey
into spaciousness.

Some Things

Some suns rise over worlds we do not yet know
because they blinked out of existence long ago
when we flitted through darkness
in search of mass, and enough gravity to fall.

Some dreams die before we can wake them.
What begins as erotic
climaxes into slaughter
and spills over borders into dangerous lands.

Some blood forgets how to dance
through vessels that branch out to carry life.
Once loosed from the body
their stains are like footprints pointing home.

Some wounds run too deep
for the light to reach them.
Those are the scars that fade to invisible
and are the softest to touch.

Some hearts suddenly remember to beat
at the moment of connection between flesh and burning flesh
between eyes and searching eyes
when it is finally safe to breathe.

Come Find Me

When this country splits in two
and falls in pieces on the hungry land
come find me and we shall plant seeds.
I am waiting.

When your chains of supply dry up
and the shelves of your store are bare
come find me and I will replenish you.
I am waiting.

When your messages go unanswered
and your pain leaves you writhing with want
come find me and we will talk in whispers and moans.
I am waiting.

Do not look for me in bytes or the binary code of ons and offs.
You will not find me in pictures or a signal humming
and crackling that sounds like my voice.
I am not waiting in a room with a lock and key, or even a door.
I am sitting here on a lily pad in our pond
clutching my chest to keep my heart inside
because it grows tired of beating.
It longs to fall into your hands
so you can squeeze it back to life.

Gravity

I am in orbit, constantly circling my pain
like the earth falling toward the sun.
Turing through cold blackness
I am tempted to let myself slow, stop and be consumed.

You are a comet who crosses my sky.
A fiery trail that burns like an after image
when I close my eyes. No tears can extinguish it.

Deep inside this planet that is me,
water drips from stalactites into
the darkness of cavern pools.
Each drop sounds out part of an answer
in an ancient code. It says that there
must be motion and that falling
is part of the journey. It whispers
of other bodies, spinning being pulled
towards their own secret centers.

You blaze passed me, certain in your position,
Draw me back just enough to trace the outer curve.
And I know there will be others.
And I know you will return.

As I am falling toward the sun
I wonder,
how long will Eternity keep saving me?

SECTION 5: I AM

Prayer to Prometheus

And now, though feeble and short-lived,
Mankind has flaming fire and therefrom learns many crafts.
~Hesiod c. 700 B.C.

Let me be a tongue of fire
dancing on the end of a blackened wick,
licking up the breath of pain
and changing it into a heated leap
of yellow and blue.

Find me a way through the darkness,
a journey from ruin
to the womb of want.

Watch me move,
driven by a hunger to find the end,
the place where light becomes a scent
that recalls honeysuckle and blood.

Surround me with a shallow pool
of clear, liquid wax that I may drip
molten memories on the hand
that gave me birth.

Teach me that I am a gift.

Season of Silence

Five was the age
when she learned about silence.
She wasn't supposed to play with you,
but you led her into the springing woods.

Your panties were white
speckled with yellow
flowers, each cotton blossom
tied with a terrible
red ribbon. Open
to the May air
you beckoned
Kiss me

here. Fingers not sufficient,
you reached
for the fallen limb
of a quiet oak.
Every creature lost

its voice. She listened
to the painful crackle
of scattered leaves
as she turned her ear
to the verdant earth.

Rhapsody on a Theme of Prostitution

During the dinner hour,
when you're supposed to be spending quality time
with the wife and kids, I'm sitting in my booth,
door locked…waiting for you…listening to Rachmaninoff
and editing a book on Buddhist philosophy
for my friend, the professor. Seven tokens open the curtain
for seven minutes. $15 to see my tits, $20 to see everything
$10 more if you want to talk. You are 21 or 86,
can cum in two minutes or barely make it in seven. You stand or sit
or sit and stand, sit and stand like a good Catholic during mass.
No, I won't meet you after my shift, even for $100,
that would be prostitution. But we can talk about it until midnight
as long as twenties keep dropping and the manager
hears tokens clinking in his clever machine.
In your side of our divided, private booth
you can't hear Hotel California repeating its warning
on the exhausted CD player…my favorite song for the show.
When I'm on the floor, my head thrown back in an illusion of ecstasy,
I dream of my lover…
When I lift my head, the curtain is closed…how long?
At the end of my shift, I put on lightly powdered rubber gloves,
clean the long drips of dried semen off your side of the glass,
change out of my work clothes and drive home.
I wonder…$375 isn't bad for a four-hour shift,
especially when I don't have to touch anyone but myself…or is it?

The Day I Gave Up on Words

It was a Friday night, nearly Saturday morning.
They came out empty, hungry, and wanting.
So many of them, like tears shed for lovers lost
or a dead sister, or a sister silenced by a cult.
They spilled and fell and covered my lips red
like the time I whispered and heard nothing in return.
They asked questions and I did not understand the answers.
They came out of my pen in throbbing, curved blue lines
that I could not read because they said nothing…meant even less.
I turned to thoughts, feelings, and experiences for knowing.
Waited breathlessly for some sign.
I am still waiting. And I am sad. And I think of death.
I experience the sacrifice of my humanity on the altar of family.
My blood gushes from an ancient wound that I am not allowed to heal
because the offering is too precious too ripe too full too late to give back
the word that commands it the sentence that damns it
to a life not worth living to a pang of birth giving
breath to an infant destine for greatness that never comes
only waits and waits and waits for words
when touch would have saved her from words
that spoke in tongues of fire dancing over heads of mutes
who know the secret, act it out in a sacred game of charades
watched by the blind who could not hear the screams
that raked their bloody throats slit open by a sword,
a Holy War against reason.
And what does this mean? What salvation does it bring?
Nothing.
Absolutely nothing.

Reaching Up…an Interpretation

After the Garden and after the Flood,
when puddles and mud crept back into seas,
after sons and daughters of families and tribes
spread Eastward into mountainous regions
and valley plains,
the Tower of Babel rose from dust.
Was it water, clay and straw
baked into bricks and sealed together with bitumen
that made it stretch its steps to touch Heaven?
Was it sweat, muscle and bone
driven by minds that had not forgotten Perfection?

What was I building,
creating from the shards of my shattered childhood,
before God confused the language
that once danced with precise art in my head?
Were God and His Holy Host afraid
that nothing I planned to do would be impossible for me?
Is that the reason He knelt down
and touched me before I could touch Him?
Perhaps.
Yet he left a trace of His path in the air and clouds and stars
as He drew Himself back into His city of pearls and gold
so that I might follow that residue of light
and still, if I am mindful and radiate compassion,
find a way to His face.

Washing the Bowls

My professor asked me to define my cultural bowls
and from how many of them I eat, what privileges draw me to
them
and what powers push me away. I obediently set about my task
read from endless journals and tomes
each one giving a different meaning for the same, simple dish.
In the end, I won all the points, understood my bowls even less,
and felt alone even more. And I contemplated suffering
and impermanence and no-self, turned them in my questioning
hands
as I washed each bowl mindfully, felt the water and the soap and
the filth
slip between each of my fingers until only the bowls remained.
So I washed them again, again, and again
until the shadow of the dirt and the shimmering of the bubbles
and the reflection in the water crept into my confused eyes
and spread across my waiting lips whispering the answer…
It is the washing that heals, the repetition that reveals…
the letting go and allowing flow, to pour through me
and swirl around me, the tears and the laughter…all at once
So I am writing the paper again, it will never be graded,
and walking beside you on the journey home.

Before and After

It was in the wee hours
when I lit the candles
called up Enya on my playlist
and spread my softest burgundy blanket
on the everyday-ness of my bed.
It was eight hours before surgery
when I lay down in that sacred place
like a spring lamb on the altar.
I sang a song to my breasts
and made love to them with reverence
until I surrendered to their ecstasy
and cried through my tears
a howling, primal goodbye.

After the moon waxed and waned
on her healing journey for all
I lifted my arms…high…to her and danced,
pounded the bareness of my feet
on the breast of Mother Earth.
turned my hips to the east and west
the hello and goodbye of Father Sun.
drummed my belly with my hands
until the rhythm came from my body,
then my soul, then my sisters, then the Source.
Finally, I called out to nothing I know,
Take anything from me
I will be as I always was,
the Feminine Divine.

Yearning

I walk the wavering wire between extremes
where the tension is high so the center can hold.
Grasp the ritual of chaos, descend into measured madness,
and the routine of folding laundry
warm from the dryer on a winter morning.

I touch the trauma and the tantra
the ripped flesh and burning pleasure.
The core wound is forever…and so is the healing.

I listen to the wail of death, gather him to my breast.
Loving the god he is, the promise he holds,
the way he paves for life…born again into wonder.

Yes, I embrace the full catastrophe of life.
And the moment before the honey
is far better than the honey itself.

The Answer

Because I am greater
than any of my problems,
I embrace my pain
and say, *Yes*.
I look into the eyes of my suffering
and say, *Thank you*.
And all the blood does not stain,
every bone finds a way to mend,
and flesh stretches to cover the wound.
Time settles back into the seas
where mystics swim
and whores kneel
before the Christ,
The Cross
and Creation
that came from the darkness
wet and wild.
The unexpected child
crystal of my empty womb
dripping
from my uneducated tongue
dropping
into the abyss that looks back at me.
And to my question, *Why?*
it answers,
Why not?

Siren Transformed

I sing to my deepest desires
a melody of Life's longing for itself...
Lure my innocent lust with images
of unscarred breasts, belly, and thighs.
My body speaks the language of water,
cleanses the wound and unbreaks the bone
with rivers of tears
falling from eyes that remember the past,
sparkle in this moment,
and see endless possibilities ahead...
Not all of them are pleasant,
yet at least they are clear.
And I choose, every day, to rise and loosen
even more, the ropes binding me
to a false sense of safety...
Preparing to defy Odysseus' command
once again...and again...and again...
'til comes the day when I no longer hear his voice.
It is the day I will learn to swim...
and add harmony to my opus.

Planet Fitness

I took a job.
I clean dried sweat droplets off gym equipment
like a Japanese tea master
drawing his katana on a bridge
before a scarred samurai.
With my left hand I hold the rag
while my right-hand sprays it with cleanser.
I mindfully watch the spray
fan its wetness against thirsty cloth.
I strap a vacuum to my back.
Clean dust, bits of paper towels, and flakes of mud off the floor.
Reach out to the sacred, stable floor with a wand.
Suck away forgotten detritus with reverence.
And I feel magnificent.
As she walks on the treadmill
Gina says, *You're not from here, are you?*
You don't do this for a paycheck, do you?
And the air shimmers with energy
linked to diligence by presence.
Everything is Self-So
and I can now die with honor.

Ordinary Miracle

Last night I asked my cat
        What is the answer, Gigi?
Looked into the expanse of her eyes,
into their total, accepting openness.
        What is it?
        Please...tell me.
She gazed back
into my begging smallness,
purred...
the sound of water in the womb...
tilted and lowered her head
toward me
with perfect grace
as if to say
        Pet me.
without the slightest apology
or explanation
as if it were
her divine birthright.

So I stroked the softness
between her offered ears
and the answer came,
not in words,
it washed through me.
And I was born...again.

Nightmare Protocol

It was vicious, gory, and I felt it.
I felt everything.
The terror and trappedness, the tearing flesh, and drip of blood.
I called and you answered,
a weary, wakened voice willing to guide
and say it was not real that I was here, not there.
A voice ready to ground in the pictures on my wall,
the softness of my purple blanket, and the cat's blinking eye
Blinking, trusting innocence.
And the voice soothed with, *Don't forget to breathe.*
And the tears flowed more slowly,
                                    Out longer than in.
sputtered wet then sparse then stopped.
And the rainstorm, laced with piano, burned in pressing drops
like a lighthouse guiding me home,
ushering me into the harbor with Aries and Taurus
and Gemini further still
Sparkling above and sleeping blossoms below
Sleeping, sleeping, sleeping.
Whispering breaths
dreaming, dreaming, dreaming
of sweetness and faeries and a stream
covered with an arched bridge leading to a one room cabin
where we all gather for the rest of the night
Safe, safe, safe.

I am the River

I do not belong
to any spiritual tradition.
I am the river
that runs through them all,
lapping at their shores
cutting across landscapes
bending in gentle beauty
rushing over loaves of stone
settling into the holy quiet
of shaded pools.
I carry them all along in my waters
and deposit them
on the delta of eternity
where we mingle in the mystery,
in the spacious ocean of infinity
until we come round again,
born like a child into a new world.
Into yet another expression
of life longing for itself.

This, Too

I move through the underworld
stick out my swollen tongue and gurgle with lust.
　　　This, too, is God.

I work in secret, with the rituals of death
and the darkness churns below my navel.
　　　This, too, is God.

I wear a necklace of skulls, throat my banshee cry of wisdom
dance naked around the fire, pound my feet in defiant mud.
　　　This, too, is God.

I tilt the spread of my hips forward and back,
side to side, until nectar drizzles down my thighs.
　　　This, too, is God.

I bite through your bones. The marrow between right and wrong
drips from my fangs and lips where Life finds its way into my
veins.
　　　This, too, is God.

I cut off my head hold it up high and drink
from the fountain of blood pulsing out of my neck.
　　　This, too, is God.

Yes, beneath the Holy of Holies is the ecstatic, carnal morass
the perfect mirror image the Other of the One, the Nothing of
the Everything.
　　　This, too, is God.

Dream

I close my eyes,
come down the Andes that are the grooves in my brain.
Enter the headwaters of the Amazon,
the river that runs through the rain forest that is my body.
deep…deep…deep
I ride in the boat of my breath going past the places that have names
into the ineffable jungle night, the raging war of life and murder
where millions of hearts beat, hang and drip and slink away
beneath the canopy of water, of leaves, of stars.

I am nothing but the embodiment of experience
the living love story
and the world God made in anger.
I hold a praying mantis on my hand.
What is going through your mind?
Death before dawn and water and blood and an anaconda
larger than the circle of my arms slipping into the great darkness
its scales and muscles and scent, beyond the jaguar kill
and the circling vultures and the thatched, grass hut
full of Life's riddle, stranger to macadam.
Women, mothers of the forest
basin…belly…womb
Giving birth to slick stillness.
Rising in a silent cry of wonder.

Creative Change

Love knows that nothing new can come until the seed has fallen
Until it is swallowed whole by the ground of being
And comes again…tender, empty…full of wonder

Love fights to remember the darkness
The place from which shadow came
And then the light

Love says the thing the Devil fears most is laughter
When invited to stay the night
To drink from the cup of want

Love feeds the hungry ghosts
The ones that do not realize they are dead
Until they are born into my embrace

Love lets go of that which I fear
Not dropping it to the cold earth
But opening the hand wide
Allowing it to rest on my palm
Visible, naked, known

I lift it up and place it against my heart

Conversation

I talk with myself
about the Answer
when I do not even understand
the Question.
It makes me cry.
And one poem
writes itself into another
like the night
bleeds into the day
leaving a wound
that refuses to heal.
A scar that will not fade,
that only stares back at me
reminding me
of when I was smooth and even,
supple and innocent.
Is the cut of wisdom
worth the loss of blood?

Recovering

The autumn air nibbles at my flesh
and reminds me of the sparkling winter to come
when the feeling of driving through the icy afternoon
is rewarded by the pleasure of crossing over the threshold
into the warmth of home.

Long walks through piles of crisp, brown leaves
with the one o'clock sun shining on my face,
and the smell of dark, rich earth
digging into my storehouse of memories.

And what I remember
is the child playing in the woods behind the country home
believing the trees were a castle, and she, a faerie queen.
Dancing around the fire pit in the clearing,
feeling roots burrow down from the bottoms of her feet
into Mama Earth, and her lovely arms sway like limbs
before the flames.

And the fire…and stones…and trees…
and the earth…and her body
sang a song of wonder at being alive.
Her mind was the music,
her heart the rhythm
beating wildly beneath the stars
that will never forget how to shine…
And neither will she.

SECTION 6: WE ARE

We Are Here

I sit with my peers and listen,
witness the rawness of their pain,
hold safe, sacred space
where they can lay down their dry bones
and drink deeply from the ordinary
clay cup of compassion,
feel embodied support and discover
their own magnificence.
I whisper,
I am here.
We are here.

For one brief moment we are in the center,
between the extremes, so that the core can hold.
We find sanctuary in seemingly insignificant acts
of courage like making our beds,
brushing our teeth, and allowing a smile
to curl our lips, a laugh to escape our throats.
We dare to love, to walk the wire without
a net of knowing, a promise of a return to innocence.
We embark on an uncertain journey,
bow our heads in silent reverence.
Yes, we are here.

I cannot understand completely
their unique suffering, but I can relate.
We know the howling loneliness that burns in the night
and trembles during the day.
We know the bite of the blade
and the warmth of the sun
that refuses to abandon our scars in darkness.
We feel the choke of pills in our throats,
day after endless day,
leaving behind effects that rival
the chemical lullaby seducing us,
calling out to us quietly,

I am here.
We are here.

What resonates with me,
like the sound of a prayer wheel spinning,
is our tireless march
straight into the arms of wellness.
Our unwavering journey home
through deep forests of ancient pain.
We walk side by side
and climb when we lose sight of the trail
never giving up hope that the path will reappear.
And we sing,
We are here.

Because we are our own shamans,
the stuff of stars vibrated into flesh,
it is our birthright to heal
the impact craters of our youth,
finding our truth…
our resilience is our brilliance
and We Are Here.

Light

An unknown number of candles
were set afloat on a river
one night.

They drifted alone,
yet closely,
and people were comforted
by their glow.

When the sun rose
all was one great light.

It was difficult
to recall the darkness.

Leap of Faith

at the bottom of the abyss comes the voice
of salvation...at the darkest moment comes the light
  ~Joseph Campbell, *The Power of Myth*

Do not be afraid of the abyss.
What you think is a monster may not be so.
Is its breath not sweet and lifted by warmth like summer
gardenias?
Fall into the break then, obey the voice
and find what waits even further below,
beyond the other side, beneath the bottom
where creative, conscious living energy pours
into space-time and breaks in two.
Male and Female, Day and Night, Birth and Death,
every duality demanding tension
so the form will hold.
Two,
always two,
of the same Oneness.
The double helix
spirals and splits and spills
across empty pages
filling them with myth and mystery and metaphor
and the waters in which mystics swim.
Fall into the break then,
you will not drown.

Mother Mary Go Round

Caught between apes and angels
humans still hunt and gather
forage through nebulas
cast aside galaxies
prey on black holes.
She brings home stories
from the raw and bloody edges of the universe
paints them on cave walls
dances their meanings around sacred, tribal fires
engraves symbols on clay tablets
then leaves it all behind, unexplained
for still distant evolutions to ponder
during their ride on the Wheel
their journey from believing to knowing
their quest for release
from the silent slipping
through the flayed fingers of gods
into the womb of what was.

Belly Wisdom

To all those who live close
Who creep or crawl or slither
Belly to the earth
The serpents and the ants the spiders
Full of dust or mud or snow
I give thanks

With gratitude I turn to the West
Where mamma stands in her apron
Hand to her belly
Dinner and stories and womb
Bearer of children and morals and fruit pies
She brings wisdom

To all those who die far away
Who march or travel or swim
In the belly of the whale
The mystics and the gypsies and the soldiers
Full of light or lust or love
I give thanks

With a sacred heart I bow my head
To the Women of the Wheel
Bellies full of emptiness
Brimming and aching and soft
Tellers of truths and loss and abundance
She brings wisdom

To all those who have transcended into Awareness
who sit or breathe or question
The answers the air and the pillows
Eternity in their bellies
Full of mastery and mystery and magic
I give thanks

Elusive Enigma

When will we stop riding the pendulum
like it was a wrecking ball
left to right, forward and back
and settle into the center where mystics and scientists
Lie close in the same bed
working mysteries in full light
reaching out and reaching in
to grab the truth and the reality.
Because life comes from pleasure
and pleasure ends in pain
where particles and waves
are one and the same.

The universe plays peek-a-boo with us
gives us the corpus callosum
to keep the hemispheres from annihilating each other.
Gives us Helen Keller
who knew no separation
between herself and the world
until she learned language.
Did she expand, contract, or shatter?
Gives us the empirical and experiential
and dares us to study, to do, to be.
Yes, we embrace the ambiguity
and the absolute truth,
cling to the words
and swim in the spaces between them.

Being Human

there is no giving it back
no unpicking it
or unbiting it

only the constant tension
between wanting to tell someone
I shouldn't have done it.
and
It tasted so good.

even the Tree's shade
becomes unbearable.
its shifting shadow
offers no lasting
concealment
and life becomes
a ceaseless search
for unknowing,
an endless wearing
of ill-fitting animal skins
that were never ours to wear

The Answerless Question

These are the things
born from profound suffering...
There is doing
There is having
And there is being
The coalescence of the three
Is the ruby-throated hummingbird
That hovers before the nectar
And does not say
Now, I will drink....
The dream of the faceless man
That.... somehow....
Looks into our eyes
And..... somehow.....
Tells us,
It is time to leave the staying
....again.

We Are

We are stained glass windows in an antiquarian church
crafted to allow divine light to pass through our colors
to illuminate, to comfort, to remind
those who have lost their way and seek sanctuary
that because things seem pointless
does not mean they are meaningless.

Our mortal, metal webs are filled with a hundred panes
which once were sand…made molten, tested by fire
cooled into beauty, fitted by the Maker's hands
into frames of stone to serve as guardians
against darkness and raging storms.

How dare we not reach up to heaven,
revel in our delicate strength,
and take our humble place among the sacred,
within the flow of centuries, beneath the eyes of God
who touches us until we tremble and teeter
on the edge of breaking.

The scene we portray,
the pattern emergent on our surface
is not nearly as important
as our purpose for being there,
a purpose that can only be found
in the eyes of those who look through us,
searching for the light that lies beyond.

Acknowledgements

Connections Literary Magazine, 1993-2024
  "A Child's Memory," "For Marietta," "Prophecies,"
  "Silences," "Surrendering," "Light," "Sweet Basil
  and Marmalade," "A Gentle Undoing" (previously titled
  "Residue of Dreams"), "No Big Loss"
  (previously titled "Rings"), "The Beekeeper's Daughters,"
  "Making Peace," "Sitting in the
  Mystery," "Gift," "February 16th," "My Offer," "Belly
  Wisdom," "Child of Glass"

Harrington Lesbian Fiction Quarterly, 2005
  "House of the Ordinary Gods," "Prophecies," "Rhapsody
  on a Theme of Prostitution," "I Have
  Told You Everything" (previously titled "The Truth of It")

The Reflector, 2010
  "A Family Narrative"

Voices Israel, 2020
  "Reaching Up…An Interpretation"

Tiny Moments, Vol IV, 2024
  "Ordinary Miracle"